HEALING - THE SHAMAN'S WAY
BOOK 7
SHAMANISM AND SPIRITUALITY

Norman W. Wilson PhD

**HEALING - THE SHAMAN'S WAY
BOOK 7
SHAMANISM AND SPIRITUALITY**

Cover Design by
S.R. Walker Designs
www.srwalkerdesigns.com

Interior Design
Omar Lopez, PhD

FICTION4ALL

A FICTION4ALL PAPERBACK

©Copyright 2025

Norman W. Wilson, PhD
The right of Norman W. Wilson to be identified as author and channel of this work has been asserted by him in accordance with the Copyright , Designs and Patents Act 1988.

All Rights Reserved

No reproduction, copy or transmission of the publication may be made without written permission.

No paragraph of this publication may be reproduced, copied, or transmitted say with the written permission of the publisher, or in accordance with the provisions of the Copyright Act 1956 (as amended).

Any person who does any unauthorized act in relation to his publication may be liable to criminal prosecution and civil claims for damages.

ISBN: 978 1 78695 901 0

Published by Fiction4All.
www.fiction4all.com
This edition published 2025

A SPECIAL THANKS TO

Stuart Holland, my publisher, for his personal attention during the completion of this work and for bringing it to the printed page.

Stephen R. Walker, my book cover designer, for his personal attention to detail and execution of design appropriate for the subject matter of this book.

Omar Lopez, PhD, my book's interior designer, for his keen insight in what best worked with the concepts presented in the textual content of this book.

Suzanne V Wilson, my wife, who has inspired, encouraged, and tolerated much during this project.

HEALING-THE SHAMAN'S WAY: SHAMANISM AND SPIRITUALITY

CHAPTER ONE

WHAT IS SHAMANISM?

Welcome to the world of shamanism and spirituality. I am a Shaman; I am not a Native American nor am I a First Nation person of Canada. However, I was trained by a Mi'kmaq healer named Elisapie. I called her Sa-pie. The Mi'kmaq word for a healer is **nepiteget**. Each Native American and First Nation tribe of Canada has its own words for a healer. Shaman is not one of them

Since the word shaman is not in the normal daily languages of local Native tribes, why do I use it? Until recently, interest in shamanism remained to those interested in ethnology, anthropology, and psychoanalysis. The late Michael Harner is credited with popularizing shamanism and its concepts. Consequently, I use the word shaman because it is within the current popular language.

If the word shaman is not from North, Central, or South American tribes where do we get the word? As with many things from antiquity, the origin of the word shaman has its challenges. There is some general agreement among etymologists that the word shaman came from the Tungus language of Siberia, specifically from the Evenki word "šaman," which means "spiritual healer" or "one who knows." Who knows what? How to help people heal themselves physically, emotionally, and spiritually.

The term was adopted into Russian in the 17th century when Peter the Great sent an envoy to China. Two Dutch diplomats, Gerrit de Veer, and Johan Nieuhof, traveled with the envoy and reported about meeting Scha-man. Their writings later entered the English and European languages. De Veer and Nieuhof were part of the Dutch East India Company's efforts to establish trade agreements with China.

In the Evenki language, "šaman" refers to a person who communicates with the spirit world, often acting as a healer or guide for their community. Over time, the term has been used more broadly to describe similar figures in various Indigenous cultures around the world.

In his book Shamanism: Archaic Techniques of Ecstasy, Mircea Eliade stated that the shaman "is a man who has immediate concrete experiences with gods and spirits...." That is not correct. Women were and are shamans. The Tungus word for female shamans is *shamanka*. Also, the word *sama* in the Tungus refers to both males and females who have achieved the necessary skills.

The notion that the word shaman is from the Tungus of Siberia is not without challenge. Some authorities claim the word comes from the Chinese word *scha-man* and others claim it's from the Pali word *schamana,* a term used for a Buddhist monk, and *sramana* from Sanskrit.

Evidence of shamanic practices suggests they are at least 40,000 years old. This evidence has been found in Paleolithic cave paintings such as those of Lascaux Cave in France (17.000 BCE) and the Altamira Cave (Spain) dating back to 36,000 BCE. Artifacts found in burial sites in Siberia, for example, have revealed carvings made of bone, drums, masks, and clothing decorated with animal imagery. Excavations in Turkey have revealed large stone pillars with carvings that suggest the area was a ceremonial center. Ancient Sumerian cuneiform tablets and Ancient Egyptian texts include those who could be called shamans.

As hundreds of years passed, shamanism showing a remarkable adaptability, gradually evolved, diverse as its forms are, into a dual concept: healing and spirituality. Because of this dual concept, the shaman took on several roles which included any one or more of the following:

- Historian
- Sage
- Healer
- Spiritualist
- Mediator

- Traveler

As a historian, the shaman sings the story of his or her people. The oral tradition meant that someone was always being taught the stories of the tribe.

The sage, just as the word suggests, is a wise man or woman; one whom the tribe leadership respects. A modern example would be an advisor or mentor.

The healer relies upon the vast medicines that populate the natural world, sound, and movement to treat his or her patients.

As a spiritualist, the shaman incorporates a deep connection between human beings and the natural world that includes animals, trees, rocks, the elements such as rain as inherent life forces. Simply, it is the notion that all things are alive.

The shaman may function as a mediator between mankind and the Spirit World and one's ancestors; between individuals and families that are in dispute.

As a traveler, the shaman moves from the current realm to another. Traditionally, there are three realms or divisions:

1. Underworld- Here emotions, memories and their psychic healing takes place
2. Middle World – Here plant spirits, spells, curses, and ghosts are located. Generally, this is just outside of ordinary reality.
3. Upper World-Spiritual teachers are located here. Jung's archetypes also exist here.

To arrive at these realms requires an altered state of consciousness, and therein, lies inherent dangers. First is the lack of trained people who provide and supervise the use of hallucinogens. Second, is the overdose of hallucinogens and third is being disrespectful of the Realms, especially the Underworld.

Three stories from ancient literature demonstrate what happens when the traveler does not follow proper protocol: Orpheus and Eurydice, Persephone and Demeter, and Gilgamesh and Enkidu.

I have to admit I have a bias when it comes to the use of hallucinogens to create a trance to go to another Realm. I don't recommend their use. There are other safer ways to create a trance state: drumming, for example.

CHAPTER TWO

SHAMANISM VS RELIGION

Understandably, some people believe Shamanism is a religion. Culturally, its practices have been the basis of what is now called religion. Among these practices are prayer, ceremonial, and sacrificial offerings.

It can be said that individuals are drawn to religion for the structure and guidance it offers through its leaders and sacred texts. The potential help from a higher power and a defined moral code is found to be attractive to many. Religion offers a sense of purpose and belonging within a spiritual framework.

Shamanism, on the other hand, is attractive to those who seek a more personal and experiential approach to life. Shamanic Practices offer a deep personal connection to the natural and spiritual worlds. Combining Shamanic Healing techniques and traditions enhances that connection. Shamanism offers a more individualized, intuitive, and spiritual path than religion. Further, the possibility of communicating with the members of the Spirit World charms those who seek spiritual help.

Most religions have a formalized structure. Included in this structure are sacred texts: Kitab-i-Aqdas (Baha'i'), Tripitaka (Buddhism), Bible (Christianity), Vedas (Hinduism), Qur'an

(Islam), (Tanakh (Judaism), and Avesta (Zoroastrianism). And then, there are the cathedrals, churches, mosques, temples, priests, rabbis, nuns, pastors, and imams.

In contrast, the shamans have been chosen and trained to fill the special role of healer, communicator with the Spirit World, and keeper of tribal history.

Religions generally have a formal belief system about a deity or deities, creation, life after death, and a set of rules of behavior. Islam has the Sharia, Hinduism has the Bhagavad Gita, and Christianity has The Ten Commandments. Shamanism focuses on a worldview in which nature, spirits, and ancestors play a key role. The spiritual realm, for the shaman, is interconnected with the natural world and as such they may directly interact with the spirits to get help or to gain knowledge. Thus, there is less standardization and more experientialism.

Religious practices, rituals, and ceremonies are more formalized and prescribed by doctrine. Prayer, fasting, feasts, and ceremonies are quite seasonal: Christmas, Diwali, and Ramadan, for example. Shamanic practices are considerably more personalized and involve altered states of consciousness created by drumming, hypnotic dancing, and or the use of hallucinogenic substances. Peyote, Psilocybin, and mushrooms.

Most of the religions of the world stress community worship, that is, coming together for special ceremonies, holy days, and congregational prayers. What happens is the development of a shared identity and a belief in a common moral code. Shamanism is individually focused. Even though the shaman's work is individually focused the role is to serve the community. Much of the shamanic work is done through a personal spiritual journey to any one of the three spiritual realms: Upper, Middle, and Lower. Vision Quests, as they are called, are to seek guidance and understanding.

The world's major religions have sacred texts that play a major role in their belief systems. Shamanism does not rely on written documentation. The knowledge is handed down from one generation to the next. The Shaman plays the role of story teller.

Religious groups' leaders have their own way of doing things. Choosing what will be the topic of a Sunday sermon, or a lecture at the Kiwanis. So too, do shamans. Individual shaman have their own methods, tools, and approaches to issues.

Despite their long history, shamans face criticism and outright condemnation. Admittedly, shamanism has been likened to a cult. Some "followers" have adopted the use of drugs such as Opium, Poppies, and Salvia Divinorum supposedly to help them with their Vision Quests. As with everything else, some diminish the value of certain aspects of living.

Some modern dictionaries have defined a shaman as a person who uses magic to cure illnesses and to control spiritual forces for ill purposes. Shamans do not typically use what is called magic. Any effort to bring harm to another is a direct violation of what a healer is all about.

It is an accepted concept that religion centers around the worship of a divinity. Gabi Kovalenko in "Religion VS Spirituality" (Be Your Own Creator) states that in religion, "God is outside of you" That is not the case with Shamanism; for the shaman, the Divine is everywhere—including inside of you whether you accept it or not. Kovalenko further reminds us that religion separates people whereas, shamanism makes no such belief distinctions. When you realize there are at least 45,00 different Christian denominations worldwide the implication of Kovalenko's statement becomes agonizingly clear. . . religion separates people.

While religions perpetuate a belief system based on other people's experiences, shamanism does not. It is personal. Religion and spirituality are often used interchangeably but that is wrong. The two concepts, as you will see, are different. Yet, do not lose sight of the fact that both religion and shamanism affirm the existence of a realm beyond the physical world. In religion, this takes the form of heaven, the afterlife, or the presence of the divine. Shamanism, involves journeys to the spirit world, communicating with spirits. Both open an involvement in the understanding of reality that extends beyond the immediate tangible material world. While religion and shamanism differ in their structures and beliefs, they both seek to address the spiritual needs of individuals and communities, offering paths to understanding, healing and a connection to the divine—whatever that may be.

CHAPTER THREE

SHAMANISM AND SPIRITUALITY

THE SHAMANIC WORLD VIEW©

The centerpiece of the shamanic worldview is the *axis mundi*—the idea or concept of a center that connects to the heavens, earth, and the underworld. Such a concept is found in many cultures and religions around the world. It can be traced from ancient Mesopotamia texts and their idea of Ziggurats.

It is claimed the ancient Egyptian pyramids connected the earth and that which was considered divine. From the Hindu and Buddhists comes the idea of the sacred mountain, Mount Meru. It was believed to be the center of everything physical and spiritual. The ancient writings called the Puranas, the Mahabharata, and the Ramayana acknowledge this center of the universe concept.

From Greek and Roman antiquity comes Mount Olympus and the Omphalos Stone, both considered the center of the world.

Even though the word axis mundi did not come into use until the 20th Century when Romanian religious historian, Mircea Eliade introduced the term in his scholarly writings.

The term, Axis Mundi is of a Latin origin and means "axis of the world." It represents the connection between the different realms of existence: Heaven, Earth, and the Underworld.

The physical representation of the Axis Mundi is often a ladder stretching skyward or as a tree; for example, Yggdrasil in ancient Norse mythology.

Five aspects of the shamanic belief system constitute the shamanic worldview.

Tenet One:

There is no need to confirm the world. For the shaman what is, is and it is a perception. Further, a perception cannot be proven or disproven.

Tenet Two:

Just as the mind and matter are intertwined, the shaman believes the Self and all else are connected. All things contain a lifeforce, a Soul or Spirit.

Tenet Three:

The shaman believes the individual is responsible for their health.

Tenet Four:

Reality is not just a physical representation. It is both an ordinary and non-ordinary reality.

Tenet Five:

By whatever name you want to call it, the world, the universe, or the cosmos, it is a living and evolving entity, continually changing.

Peggy Malnati reminds us that "reality is perceived as being layered rather than flat and single-dimensional. Existence is not only perceived as being layered in parallel and overlapping horizontal dimensions but also it is layered vertically." ("The Shamanic View of the World. Walksoftly2's Blog. 2011) Included are a variety of spiritual aspects that are central to shamanic practices and beliefs.

Within this layering, the shamanic worldview contains three levels or Realms: Heaven, Middle, and Lower. I have dropped the word Heaven and called it the Upper Realm. I have done this to avoid any religious connection or connotation, especially to the Christian religion which

The Upper Realm:

The Upper Realm is the home of teachers, ascended ones, souls of deceased humans, and Spirits that are considered safe so humans interact with them.

The Middle Realm:

The Middle Realm contains human spirits that have not been released, that is, they are still earthbound. That is, they have not crossed over. This realm is just outside the current reality in which we live. Here you will find ghosts, the souls of loved ones, and that includes pets.

The Lower Realm:

The Lower Realm is the earth. Actually, it's under the ground and it is the area of nature spirits, animal spirits, and what is commonly called 'lost souls.' Sometimes, the inhabitants of this realm are not always cooperative. A shaman would travel to this realm to find out what herbs and plants should be used in the treatment of a client.

Contemporary writings use Journeying, Traveling, Hedgecrossing, and Walking when discussing movement between the Realms. Sara Anne Lawless who uses the words 'walking between worlds' rather than journeying or traveling makes a valuable clarification. She wrote, ". . . visualization and guided meditations are NOT walking between worlds or trance work—they're painting a lovely picture of doing so in your head."(Walking Between Worlds. June 18, 2010. *Witchcraft & Muses.)* There is a personal physical movement into the Realms.

The intent here is not to teach you how to travel to another realm but to provide background. It is not a necessary requirement that you travel to another realm or dimension to find your spirituality. After all, spirituality, in a non-religious sense, as it is used here, refers to something greater than the traditional oneself—one's inner self and its connection to the natural world and that which is more than.

CHAPTER FOUR

BLACK, WHITE, AND YELLOW SHAMAN

The following material is generally considered outside of the normal classification of shamans. Because, it is relatively new, having been introduced in the early 1900s by Russian ethnographer and anthropologist, Vladimir Bogoraz who spent a good deal of time studying the Chukchi of Siberia.

Even though there is room for questioning Bogoraz's interpretation, it appears to be gaining some degree of universal recognition and therefore should be included in this course.

First and foremost, Black, Yellow, and White are not racial as in today's world and second, they do not represent bad, good, or evil. Nor does their order indicate any importance. Yet, the color designations raise questions: For some, black suggests an evil connotation, and yellow suggests an inferior quality of shamanism.

Traditionally, the **Black Shaman** was viewed as the warrior shaman. Fighters of evil, the Black Shamans are also the role models of bravery and courage. Like all shamans, the Black Shaman fulfills several roles. In times of war or natural disasters, the Black Shaman boosted the morale of the warriors as well as the tribe by conducting special ceremonies. Hunting, healing, and protection rituals, served as advisors and managed the tribe's foreign policy.

Yellow Shamanism refers to a specific type of shamanic practice in the areas of Mongolia and China. There is some confusion about the basic origin of Yellow Shamanism. Some agreement exists that suggests it came about as a division or spin-off from White Shamanism. At some point during the 16th century, Tibetan Buddhism began to have an influence in Mongolia. With this imposition of Lamaism, shamanism experienced a very difficult time.

A group of shamans succumbed to Tibetan influence causing a rift in traditional shamanism. Those who followed the Tibetans were called Yellow Shaman. Eventually, there was an integration and co-existence emerged.

As with Black Shamans, the Yellow Shamans hold several roles. Among these are being an intermediary between the physical and spiritual worlds. They performed ceremonies for healing, guidance, and asking for help in the world of spirits, and divination.

Divination was a useful Yellow Shaman technique to gain insight into the future or to come to an understanding of the causes of misfortune and to gain hidden truths. Various methods, such as casting the stones, and interpreting signs such as finding a bird's feather.

White shamans did not accept the Tibetan Buddhist influence and struggled to maintain traditional shamanic practices. They maintained the use of traditional artifacts and ceremonial objects—those things that had symbolic meanings. Among these were masks, drums, clothing, ritual knives, and figurines. Altars were important for certain rituals and used to appease and or honor spirits. Finally, one of the most important things a White Shaman, or any shaman for that matter does is to pray to the Spirits. Here is an example of such a prayer in Mongolian and in English:

"Сүнсүүдийн ном"
("Sünsiidiin nom")

"Аглаг эрхэм буянтай, тэнгэрийн эзэд ээ,
Амьдралд минь халхавчид,
хамгаалагчид аа,
Хайрлаач, өршөөнө үү, миний мөргөлд,
Гаргуулахын тулд түмний сайн сайхныг хүсэж,
Би уучлал хүсье, ихийг өгнө."

The English translation follows.

English Translation:

**"O Mighty and Beneficent Spirits of the Heavens,
Guardians and Protectors of my life,
Please have mercy and heed my prayer,**

**With the desire to bring goodness to all beings,
I seek forgiveness and offer my utmost respect."**

What does this short but powerful prayer mean? It seeks benevolence and protection from the Spirit World. For that, the shaman promises to help others and bring positive outcomes through their spiritual endeavors. The speaker ends by seeking forgiveness and offering respect.

Prayers, such as the example, are usually sung.

Dr. Joseph Ayo Fatubarin in writing about the environment states "There is an additional environment which has not sufficiently registered into the consciousness of most people." Continuing, he states, "This is partly so because it is abstract in nature and partly because it is extra-terrestrial in nature—occurring within the spiritual realm"

With the popularization of different healing modalities such as shamanic healing, there has been an increase in the spirit world and spirituality. To that end, an example of this increased interest is the creation and inclusion of sacred altars—a spiritual atmosphere and an open environment—one that is available to everyone, irrespective of religious beliefs or lack thereof.

What exactly is a sacred altar? According to Wikipedia "An altar is a table or platform for the presentation of ritualistic purposes." Altars are found in crystal shops, essential oil shops, yoga studios, and in private homes. They range from simple to complex and elaborate.

What is involved in the creation of an altar is need, intention, space, and personal taste. The following activity is only a suggestion.

ACTIVITY ONE

What You Will Need:

- A table, shelf, or top of a file cabinet
- Crystals for their spiritual qualities and enhance your intention
- Feathers (I prefer those that I find over those that are purchased)
- A drum (small)
- Rattle
- Two to 5 candles (Because of potential fire hazards, I recommend battery-operated candles
- Incense (Lavender, Frankincense-Myrrh, White Sage are suggested)
- Images or Statues (Representative of your spirit animals)
- Nature (Leaves, sea shells, small piece of driftwood, or a piece of a tree branch)
- Offering Bowl or a Fire Bowl (The offering bowl can be a small glass saucer; whereas, the fire bowl must be of a high-grade ceramic)

- Cloth (to cover the table. Shelf, file cabinet top)
- Smudge Material (White Sage, Palo Santos)
- Lighter or matches
- Small strips of white paper (Large enough to write an intention)

Directions:

- Select a quiet place
- The area should have low lighting
- Cleanse all the materials and table by smudging them with a white sage bundle.
- Place the cloth on the table
- Arrange the materials on the table

Once you are satisfied with your arrangement, take one strip of paper, write your intention for the altar, fold it, place it in the fire-proof bowl, and light it. Sit or stand quietly for a few minutes.

CHAPTER FIVE

RELIGION

The purpose here is to define and explain. It is not intended to be nor is it a criticism of any religion. With that said, what then, is religion? According to Chatgpt.com "Religion can be defined as a set of organized beliefs, and systems that often involve the worship of a higher power or deity.

A brief overview of religious history provides background for the consideration of spirituality.

Using the definition, that religion is a set of organized beliefs and systems that often involve the worship of a higher power or deity" we find an interesting history. It reveals that as civilizations arose in Mesopotamia, Egypt, the Indus Valley, and China, so too, did organized religions. Concrete evidence supports the contention that the Sumerians, Egyptians, and later both the Greeks and Romans, had very complex gods aligned with elaborate rituals; for example, the ancient Epic of Gilgamesh and t*he Pyramid Texts.*

Hinduism from ancient India emerged as one of the oldest organized religions. It is dated around 6,000 BCE. Buddhism founded by Siddhartha Gautama is about 2500 years old.

Zoroastrianism, founded by Zarathustra, came from Ancient Persia (Iran) about 4,000 years ago. It is centered around the idea of a supreme god, good vs evil, and influenced the emerging religion of Judaism.

Judaism took shape as a distinct religion around the 6th Century BCE. Expanding the concept of monotheism, and codifying ancient texts into the Tanakh, Judaism's Holy book.

Islam, founded in the 7th century CE, combined religious, legal, and social aspects of life into its holy book, the Quran.

Christianity emerged in the 1st Century CE and using texts written by followers of Jesus Christ, established what is now known as the Bible, a collection of moral and ethical behaviors.

Generally, all of these religions include the following ten special considerations or something with close similarities:

1. Divinity- Usually involves a formal structure, and has established doctrines that membership and leadership are expected to accept and follow. Among these will be sacred texts, specific rituals, and ceremonies.

2. Personal Transformation-Certainly includes acceptance of specific religious principles, ceremonies such as baptism, prayers, and active participation.

3. Transcendence- generally refers to going beyond the ordinary limits of human experiences and or understanding. This usually relates

to the divine or ultimate reality. For example, in Hinduism
and Buddhism, transcendence is associated with reaching a state of nirvana.

4. Sacred Texts- Many of the world's religions have sacred texts or scriptures. In addition to the Tanakh, Bible, Qur'an, and Vedas, there is at least a half-dozen other texts.
5. Rituals-As well as ceremonies are basic to many religions. Baptisms, marriage ceremonies, burials, and communion are just a few examples.

6. Community-Is often a primary function of religion providing shared beliefs and support.

7. Moral Guidance is offered by many religions by providing a living framework for a life based on good ethics and morality. Do no harm; do right exemplifies such morality.

8. Direct Mystical Experience-Includes direct, personal experiences of the divine, and sacred. Involved are contemplative practices.

9. Purpose and Meaning of Existence- Closely aligned with metaphysical questions dealing with existence, purpose, and meaning of life.

10. Healing-In many religions an aim is to bring about healing physically and emotionally through prayer, meditation, or rituals that are inner-peace and balance-based.

For the religious (those who attend a religious function regularly) the healing offered is regarded as spiritual. However, some do not. For example, SBNA (spiritual but not religious) people do not regard organized religion as the only means of furthering one's spiritual growth. This becomes even more significant when approximately 20% of the world's population is no longer affiliated with any religion.

Gabi Kovalenko in "Religion vs Spirituality" states "Religion is based on others' experience" and Richa Tiwari appears to agree with her when she states "Religion is rooted in the teachings and lives of historical figures, passed down through scriptures and traditions." It is not spiritual-based. What then is spirituality?

CHAPTER SIX

DEFINING SPIRITUALITY

Spirituality is something that is debated and generally misunderstood. It is all too often confused with religion. Unquestionably, spirituality is an important part of one's religious beliefs. One can be spiritual without being religious. Religion, no matter which one or division is a specific set of organized beliefs and practices shared by like-minded people. Spirituality, on the other hand, is more a personal, and private practice. One may be religious and spiritual but being one doesn't necessarily make you the other.

There are twelve classifications of spirituality:

1. **Authoritarian Spirituality** is one that places emphasis on strict adherence to religious doctrines or spiritual authorities. However, it should be noted that its followers may prioritize obedience and conformity

to those authorities' teachings and practices.

2. **Eclectic Spirituality** draws from various spiritual traditions and practices to create a personalized approach. Followers can blend ideas from religions, philosophies, and or spiritual practices to meet their personal needs.

3. **Humanistic Spirituality** emphasizes human potential and the development of personal virtues and values. Frequently, the focus is on self-improvement, psychological growth, and the cultivation of personal positive qualities. Among these qualities are compassion, integrity, and wisdom.

4. **Integral Spirituality** is an attempt to integrate multiple dimensions and facets of human experience. This includes physical, emotional, and mental aspects of human existence. It is a holistic approach including practices, beliefs, and insights from various spiritual traditions. Its aim is

a comprehensive understanding of spiritual development.

5. **Mystical Spirituality** focuses on direct personal experiences of the transcendent. It often involves meditation and contemplation. It emphasizes mystical experiences that are aimed at achieving a profound connection with a higher power and or ultimate reality.

6. **Nature-based spirituality** emphasizes a deep connection with the natural world. It involves practices that honor the Earth. These include eco-spirituality, animism, and earth worship. It views nature as sacred and as such involves rituals and practices that celebrate the earth's natural cycles.

7. **Philosophical Spirituality** focuses on the integration of spiritual insights with philosophical reflections. Often involved is the exploration of existential questions such as what is the meaning of life, what is my true essence, or what is my purpose? Through a combination of spiritual

and philosophical inquiry, it explores the nature of reality.
8. **Secular Spirituality** has its main focus on spiritual or existential concerns and these do not necessarily involve adhering to traditional religious frameworks. Practices such a mindfulness, meditation, and developing a sense of awe from a non-religious or humanistic viewpoint.
9. **Service-oriented spirituality** focuses on serving others and contributing to the well-being of community or world-based charities. It emphasizes compassion, altruism, and humanitarian efforts.

10. **Shamanic Spirituality** is a very distinct form of spiritual practice because it is based on various traditions of indigenous cultures around the world. Typically, it relies upon certain practices and beliefs that are centered on the role of the shaman's interactions with the spirit world.

11. **Social Spirituality** places emphasis on the communal and relational aspects of spiritual life. It focuses on building personal connections, fostering community, and participating in collective practices. There is a valuing of group activities and rituals. Pushes social justice efforts. It sees spirituality as that which thrives in social interaction and collective action.

12. **Transcendental Spirituality** attempts to go beyond ordinary experiences to reach higher states of consciousness. Its practices are designed to move one beyond the ego and to achieve a sense of unity with a greater reality. To help one move beyond the ego of those involved with Transcendental Spirituality it is suggested one follow the "Who am I?" popularized by Raman Maharshi.

Once again, it is not necessary to belong to any of these suggested twelve types of groups. Spirituality's focus is often on healing. Here are ten practices or activities that help promote well-being, self-discovery, and inner peace. Their goal is to balance mind, body, and spirit. Typically, they are holistic.

- <u>Breathing Exercises</u> such as deep breathing, pranayama, or any other breathing practice help to calm the mind and reduce stress.
- <u>Community and Connection</u> involves building and maintaining support-based relationships that foster a sense of belonging and spirituality.
- <u>Creative Expression</u> involves participating in creative activities: painting, music, and dance that foster a sense of fulfillment.
- <u>Gratitude</u> requires regular acknowledgment and appreciation of your being and what you are grateful for. Such activity shifts your perspective to one that enhances your overall well-being.
- <u>Journaling</u>, even though it can be time-consuming, it provides a natural release for your personal thoughts, feelings, and experiences. It can offer you clarity, positive self-

reflection as well as emotional release.

- <u>Meditation and Mindfulness Practices</u> take you into focusing your mind and staying in the present moment. It helps reduce stress and increase your self-awareness and your inner peace.
- <u>Mindful Eating</u> is not about dieting either to lose or gain weight. YOU are to be aware of what and how you eat and how that connects to your body. Simply put, it's self-care.
- <u>Nature Connection</u> is one of my favorites. Spend time in nature by hiking, biking, gardening, or watching a heart-felt sunrise or a sense of peace with a sunset. Go ahead, hug a tree.
- <u>Physical Movement</u> from my perspective does not necessarily mean jogging, on the treadmill for 60 minutes, or walking 5,000 steps daily. It can mean doing yoga, tai chi or qigong to not only integrate physical movement with breathing

but to promote balance and inner harmony.
- <u>Self-care</u> involves doing those activities that nurture your body and mind such as taking a scented bath, practicing relaxation techniques, or having a cup of herbal tea.

Why do people practice spirituality? Probably the reason why many people become involved in questing spirituality is they view it as a way to bring solace and inner peace into their life. Another reason for people getting involved with spirituality is that is often practiced alongside yoga, Qigong, and Tai Chi. Other people view spirituality as a way of coping with daily life.

ACTIVITY

UJJAYI BREATHING

The word ujjayi is Sanskrit and is derived from the sacred Hindu city of Ujjain. Ujjayi is pronounced as "**ooh-JAI-yee**." It has three syllables. The "ooh" is like the oo in the word "room. The Jai rhymes with "tie and yee rhymes with tea. Used in yoga, meditation, and concentration classes. Also called Ocean Breath, it helps relieve stress, depression, and sleep disturbances and improves concentration.

According to the National Library of Medicine, Ujjayi Breathing involves both inhalation and exhalation. Both are done through the nose. However, some authorities suggest a different approach. Both are covered in the following set of directions:

- ➢ As you inhale through your nose, using your diaphragm, keep your mouth closed
- ➢ Constrict your throat enough so your breathing makes a rushing of air sound (some call this the sound of the ocean)
- ➢ Keep your inhalations and exhalations equal in duration

Alternate Method:

- ➢ Inhale through your nose, keeping your mouth closed

- Open your mouth and exhale with some force as you say out loud, "HA."

Whichever approach you select, begin for a 5-minute duration. Do this every day for a week either in the morning or at bedtime. As you practice, gradually add time until you reach a full 10 minutes. If you feel the need to reduce the number of days you do the Ujjayi, do so. Calming, and less stress should be your reward, and just maybe you have opened the doors for shamanic spirituality the focus of the next module.

CHAPTER SEVEN

SHAMANIC SPIRITUALITY

Before we move into shamanic spirituality two terms need to be clarified: spiritualism and spirituality.

Spiritualism is a specific religious movement that has its roots in the 19th century and this is particularly true for the United States and England. Sisters, Margaret, and Kate Fox are said to be the founders. Spiritualism is based on the belief that the living can communicate with the dead through mediums. Involved are practices such as seances and table tapping, card readings, and tea leaves,

Worldwide membership is estimated to be in the hundreds of thousands.

Spirituality is a much broader and individualistic concept and has been around longer than any organized religion. Generally, it refers to a personal sense of connection that which is greater than humankind. Some call this the Universe, a higher power, or a sense of personal inner peace. On the other hand, shamanic spirituality emphasizes direct interaction with the spirit world.

In addition to interaction with the spirit world, spirituality involves the capacity for transcendence and to enter a heightened spiritual state of consciousness.

Furthermore, shamanic spirituality is more community-oriented and nature-focused

In keeping with the shamanic world of spirituality and as we begin its
discussion, I offer the following prayer. It is a traditional Native American prayer reflecting common themes found in various North American tribes. Its author is unknown.

Great Spirit, Source of all life,

I call upon you with respect and reverence.

Guide me on this sacred journey,

As I seek wisdom and healing.

Ancestors, Wise Ones of the Earth, and Sky,

I honor your presence and ask for your guidance.

Help me to see with clarity,

To hear the whispers of the wind

And to feel the heartbeat of our mother, the Earth

illuminated by your light.

And my spirit
strengthened by your wisdom.

With gratitude, I offer my
heart and prayers.,

In harmony with all that is
sacred and true.

So be it!

A slight digression: This prayer reflects a theme common to shamanic practices. First, it honors that which is considered as the source of all. It seeks advice and guidance from the author's spirit guides and in keeping with correct protocol, it expresses gratitude. For me, it is to design or to align the speaker with the spiritual. Embedded is the secret of all secrets when dealing with the Upper Realm, the Spirit Worlds, and or the Universe. The speaker uses the declarative sentence: "Guide me," and "Help me," are examples of the declarative mode. The speaker is not begging, but rather, is making a command. Note also that the speaker is not rude.

A fundamental aspect of shamanic spirituality is indeed the belief that the world is inhabited by spirits—human, animal, and vegetable—that influence the physical world. Further, these spirits can be sought out for guidance and healing. The basis for this belief is the acceptance that all things are alive including rivers, oceans, lakes, and all other aspects of the earth.

To foster and implement a natural sense of spirituality, the shaman willingly subjects himself to the following:

1. Meditation
2. Mindfulness
3. Reflection
4. Self-Inquiry

My teacher did not use these words. They are modern. What follows is an attempt to explain them from a shaman's point of view. Please bear in mind, that they are a part of being a spiritual being.

Meditation is being quiet and removing the all too often self-important I. Meditation is a perfect segue to mindfulness.

Mindfulness is being aware of your thoughts. DO NOT linger or develop a thought as it comes to mind. Let it go. Don't let the thought or emotion control you. Awareness reduces the influence of the ego,—that bossy and demanding I. The result will be a sense of unity, a sense of oneness.

Reflection Involves thinking about your understanding of the nature of the Self and the ego. This may include reading passages from sacred texts and or jotting down your thoughts about that which is. This is a natural way to lead into deep self-inquiry.

Self-Inquiry involves taking a long and penetrating look at the nature of the self; that is, your personal self. It involves these questions: Whom am I? What do I believe? What is my purpose? You may want to seek a counselor to help guide you through this.

ACTIVITY

What You Will Need:

Something that will allow you to listen to music

A quiet place to sit either in the Lotus Pose or in a comfortable chair.

A selection of quiet music at least 15 minutes in length.

Directions:

Once you are comfortable, turn on the music. Be sure it's not too loud.

As the music plays, take 5 deep breaths. Do this until the music stops.

Sit quietly for 10 to 15 minutes.

Note: You can apply these same steps to meditation, mindfulness, reflection, and self-inquiry.

Shamanic Spirituality includes nature-based living experiences such as special ceremonies that are environmentally inclusive. Before sharing some things, you can do, I want to make a brief comment about doing a Vision Quest, something that is being popularized and not always in the best interest of the participants. The fundamental function or purpose of the vision quest is not necessarily spiritual. It is defining one's life's journey.

Here, then, are four suggestions you can do to enrich your spirituality:

- **Nature Taking** a nature walk is another way in which spirituality comes into play. During the walk, keep your pace comfortably slow. Humming provides an extra edge to clearing your mind. Stop frequently, listen, look around take a deep breath, and exhale with some force.
- **Drumming and Drumming Circles-** There are many kinds of drums available. If you live in an area of high humidity or very low humidity, consider a drum that is not made of animal skin. It is recommended that a hand-held drum be used. If you

drum by yourself, keep the beat slow and easy. If possible, go outside. Drumming circles exist in many areas and offer group sessions.

- **Water**- Go to any body of water: Ocean, Lake, River, Stream, and or Pond. Take a flower or small branch from a tree in your yard. (Buy a flower if you don't grow them) Sit down. Do deep breathing 5 times. Listen for water sounds. Lean back onto the ground. Do a body stretch. Look up at the sky allowing the water sounds to connect with you. Stay put for 5 minutes. Slowly slit up. Off the water your flower or tree branch gift. As it floats away, hum.
- **Tea-**Select your tea. I recommend chamomile or lavender. Next, choose a place to enjoy your tea. If the weather permits, go outside. Have a small table. Place 3 candles on the table. I suggest using the battery type rather than those that have a flame. It's a caution just in case you fall asleep. Turn on some soft jazz music.

Boil enough water for one full cup. Heat the teapot, and pour in the boiling water. Add the tea. While the tea steeps, warm your cup. Carefully, pour the hot tea into the cup. Sit down, and take 5 breaths. Slowly sip the tea. Relax. Take in your surroundings.

That's it. WELL, NOT QUITE. What is your intention? A specific intention is very important. I suggest you write it down and place it under the teapot. An intention might be something like this: "Mind, body, soul, and heart open to all that is love."

CHAPTER EIGHT

SHAMANIC SPIRITUALITY, CRYSTALS, AND THIRD EYE

Crystals have been and are often used as healing tools, as an aid to divination, and as enhancement of spiritual practices. Additionally, it is believed crystals' unique properties amplify one's intentions, facilitate connections with one's spirit guides, and offer protection to the traveler during a journey. Please note that early mankind did not use the word crystal. To them, they were stones.

There are at least six major roles crystals have in shamanic spirituality:

- Healing
- Protection
- Divination
- Energy
- Nature
- Journeying

It is believed certain crystals have healing qualities for physical, mental, and emotional issues, and that they can balance one's energy levels and give support to the natural healing processes:

Healing:
    Amethyst—calms
    Clear Quartz—the master healer
    Larimar—emotional issues
    Rose Quartz—emotional healing and self-love
    Selenite—purifies the body

Energy:
    Citrine-—amplifies energy
    Clear Quartz—master energizer
    Orange Calcite—it vibration increase energy,
    Carnelian—boosts self-esteem, physical energy
    Calcedony—Sooths mind, body, and spirit

Protection:
    Black Tourmaline—cleanses, encourages spiritual growth
    Obsidian—releases spiritual blockages
    Tiger's Eye—helps spiritual stability

Labradorite—provides insight into one's spiritual purposes
Citrine—promotes serenity and spiritual well-being

Nature:
Green Aventurine—promotes harmony and earth connection
Malachite—connects the natural world, spiritual transformation
Moss Agate—encourages tranquility, new beginnings
Jade—nature's healer for aches and pains
Hematite—grounding, connects the spiritual realm

Divination:
Clear Quartz—spiritual growth, connects all chakras
Labradorite—aids astral travel, protects against negativity
Lapis Lazuli—promotes inner vision, strength
Fluorite—promotes clarity, stabilizes
Sodalite—aids intuition, earthly energy

Journeying:

Fluorite—harmony and clarity
Selenite—helps connect to higher realms
Moonstone—encourages safe travel to the different realms
Malachite—helps identify the journey's intention
Tourmaline—removes physical and spiritual blockages.

In addition to offering healing in various ways, crystals play a significant role in the spiritual aspects of the human being. Among these is the world of the Third Eye.

The Third Eye and Spirituality

The whole idea of the third eye is not based on scientific evidence; however, as a concept, it has been around for a very long time, especially throughout religious traditions found in Taoism, Buddhism, and Hinduism. It is estimated that the Third Eye concept extends back at least two millennia.

Also known as the "Seat of the Soul," the Third Eye refers to a center of energy that exists between the eyebrows. Connecting to the Third Eye can offer profound spiritual experiences. This connection can be made by activating the pineal gland. According to Hindu tradition, the Third Eye is represented by a Tilaka, a small mark at the center of the lower forehead. For me, that places the Third Eye in the center of the two eyebrows. The exact location may vary slightly from person to person.

Opening the Third Eye offers certain health benefits. It can deepen your spiritual connections, strengthen your intuition, , and improve your general mental and emotional intelligence. According to Griff Willams of the British School of Meditation, "Opening your Third Eye can also improve your creativity, imagination and focus." And your spirituality.

Here are five suggestions you can use to open your Third Eye:

1. Yoga Pose called Child's Pose. Helps stimulate the Pineal Gland and thus opens the Third Eye
2. Breathing Practice can aid the opening of the Third Eye. Here are 6 types of breathing practices:
3. Coherent Breathing= Breathing at about 5 breaths per minute
    a. Box Breathing-Consists of 4 equal parts: inhaling, holding the breath, exhaling, and holding the breath
    b. 4-7-8 Breathing-Involves inhaling through the nose for a count of four, holding the breath for a count of 7, and exhaling through the mouth for a count of 8
    c. 3-part Breathing-involves three distinct phrases: abdominal breathing, chest breathing, and full breath combining both, and
    d. Diaphragmatic breathing focuses on using the

diaphragm effectively. Your belly should expand
   e. Alternate Nostril Breathing involves closing one nostril while inhaling through the other and switching to exhaling through the opposite nostril.
4. Visualization Techniques involve imagining your Third Eye opening. This technique includes the following steps:
   a. Close your eyes
   b. Visualize a golden ball of light floating in the air
   c. Move the ball to the center of your forehead.
   d. Imagine this golden ball getting brighter, larger, and filling you with a clarity you have not experienced before.
5. Meditation's calming effect works well to allow the Third Eye to open. During your meditation remember to not dwell on any thought; let it go. Imagine a soft blue light flowing from the top of your head and

bathing your whole body. Once the light hits your feet, allow your Third Eye to open as if you were walking into an open field.
6. Voice is pretty much a standard in many meditation, yoga, and relaxation methods. It quietly puts you in a mild self-hypnotic state. Some experts suggest humming. I prefer using OM. Let the sound extend outward as it vibrates against the back of your throat. This may require 15 minutes.
7. Crystals can add a calming effect, and enhance your spiritual life. The list at the beginning of this course is suggested for specific areas of healing. Hold the crystal in your hand, place it over your heart, or if you are on your back, place it on your forehead.

How do you know if your Third Eye is open and active? There may be many ways to recognize an open Third Eye but here at least, are 9 ways by which you will know if you have opened your Third Eye.

- Clarity in Thought—You might sense clearer thinking and even a stronger sense of direction in your life
- Emotional Shifts—Old fears and things that caused you anxiety disappear
- Enhanced Creativity—You may experience an increase in creativity and be inspired by the natural world
- Heightened Intuition—You realize your instincts are stronger
- Increased Awareness—You tune into your surroundings with a deeper feeling of being connected with the world
- Meditative Experiences—During meditation you may feel sensations in the Third Eye area
- Physical Sensations—Sensations in the Third Eye area strengthen to the point that you find yourself wiping your forehead.
- Dreams—Dreams may be more vivid or you might experience spontaneous prophetic visualizations

- Synchronicities—You experience coincidences of events that guide you.

A note of caution: You need to approach any of these suggested signs with an open mind and a bit of skepticism. Remember, each individual's experience is unique and your Third Eye journey is spiritual personal and unique to you.

CHAPTER NINE

SPIRITUALITY AND SOUND

Spirituality is the essence of that which is inner aligned with body, spirit, and soul. Unlike many of today's religious institutions, spirituality is not dependent upon a belief system based on a deity or deities. It is a sense, a feeling of wonderment, of being one with all that is. It does not mean that you have to be jumping up and down in joy and happiness twenty-four hours a day and seven days a week.

We have discussed quieting the mind, using breathing exercises, and crystals. Implied has been the use of sound. In this module, we will bring specific uses of sound for enhancing one's spirituality.

Sound has the power to transcend the ordinary, facilitating deeper connections with oneself, others, and that which is. Sound is a bridge between the mundane and the extraordinary when it facilitates a deeper understanding of oneself and that self's place in the universe.

Ultimately, the best sounds are those that resonate with you on a personal level—those sounds that enhance your unique spiritual journey. It may be necessary to experiment with different sounds to determine which sounds you feel are most uplifting and which are not. Sounds are transformative and because they are you should take your time in selecting your sounds.

The amount of time you should spend with sounds that are designed to enhance your spiritual experiences may vary. After all, it is based on your preferences.

However, despite the emphasis on personal preferences, there are some sounds we recommend you should not use. Among these unacceptable sounds are the following:

- ✓ Loud, jarring noises that are sudden and unexpected. Among these are sirens, construction equipment

clanking, and a blast of a horn blowing
- ✓ Background noises such as loud conversations, the rumble of traffic, the beeping of electronics
- ✓ Disruptive music such as the heavy beats from a vehicle passing by, aggressive lyrics, overly fast tempos
- ✓ Constant unpleasant sounds such as dripping faucets, buzzing electronics, dogs barking, small children screeching
- ✓ Dark music that evokes feelings of sadness, fear, anger, despair, hopelessness
- ✓ Heavy bass distortion that overwhelms the senses and prevents clarity of thought, and
- ✓ High-pitched noises such as alarms, squeaky toys, someone learning to play a flute,

The significance of this list is a strong reminder that all spiritual practices involve and require a minimizing of these disruptive sounds. So, what can you do to create an appropriate space for spirituality? Even though I just listed 7 annoying sounds, there is much more to creating a space for spirituality than sound control. Following are specific suggestions for creating and maintaining a spiritual place:

- Lighting—Use soft, warm lights or natural light (no glaring sunshine). If your space has ceiling lights, turn them off, and add a dimmable lamp or a few dimmable candles. No real flammable candles. Fire potential.
- Aromatherapy—To continue setting the spiritual place, add some incense that promotes relaxation. Essential oils in a diffuser is an excellent way of maintaining a spiritual atmosphere. Lavender, Sandalwood, or Frankincense, or Palo Santo. Add 5 drops of any one of these to the diffuser. You can combine two or more.
- Seating—Make sure that whatever you choose is comfortable be it chairs, cushions, or mats.
- Clutter—Get rid of the clutter. Make sure the space is clean and things are organized. Take care that the

area doesn't look sterile by being overly organized.

- Nature Inside—A couple of plants, and a small fountain would add to the ambiance.
- Personal—Items that have special personal meaning could be included as long as they do not clutter
- Altar—Create an altar on a small stand, on a bookcase, or the floor in a corner of the room. Add your favorite crystals and a candle (battery).
- Soundproofing—To minimize external noise add a rug, and curtains. If it's within your means, add soundproofing panels.
- Temperature—Controlling the temperature if you are inside is crucial. Being too hot or too cold may hinder your spiritual session.
- Decoration—Interior as well as exterior decorations should not be a distraction. Choose soft colors, statuary should not be dominant, and crystals should not be clumped together.

- Electronics—Should be kept to a minimum. No cell phones.

Today's upside-down violent world can and does cause people to struggle with their sense of spirituality. They feel and sense a loss. If you are experiencing this feeling of personal emptiness the following approaches to spirituality may help you re-experience or develop a renewed sense of spirituality. Consider trying several of these approaches to find your comfort zone and one that works for you.

Approach One: Consider these spiritually physical practices: First, Traditional yoga is a group of <u>physical</u>, <u>mental</u>, and <u>spiritual</u> practices or disciplines that originated in <u>ancient India</u>, aimed at controlling body and mind.

Second, Qi gong offers a coordinated body posture and movement, breathing exercises, and meditation. It is useful for the purposes of health, spirituality, and martial arts training.

Third, Tai chi, an ancient Chinese martial art program has evolved into a gentle and low-impact exercise with deep breathing.

Mindfulness: Is a mental state achieved by focusing one's awareness on the present moment. One acknowledges and accepts one's feelings, thoughts, and the body's physical sensations. Letting go best describes the technique.

Guided Sessions: Participation in guided meditation sessions helps keep your focus in place. Check to see if there are local meditation centers that offer guided sessions. Such sessions are available on the Internet and Mp3 and Mp4 files. There are spiritual retreats or workshops available. Make sure that the persons doing these retreats and or workshops are certified experienced practitioners.

Community Groups: Check local community or senior centers that may offer free group meetings for meditation, spirituality, and lectures. Check the Internet for local spiritual activities.

Professional Guidance: Check your local area for professional spiritual counselors, therapists, and or life coaches.

Here are a few sound suggestions you can use to help enhance your spirituality. They are YouTube videos.

Powerful spiritual frequency - protection, wealth, miracles and blessings without limit 777

https://www.youtube.com/watch?v=VArWZSlBtro

Music of Angels and Archangels • Heal All the Damage of the Body, the Soul and the Spirit, 432Hz

https://www.youtube.com/watch?v=iXkXit4iwkM

YOUR PINEAL GLAND WILL START VIBRATING AFTER 3 MIN (963Hz GOD Frequency)

https://www.youtube.com/watch?v=WoJQ_LAzJVw

Armen Miran & Hraach-Karahunj (The Prelude)

https://www.youtube.com/watch?v=RiLe43yIONI&list=PL0J_ljJymJ9kpPpWEK7K3kDG_rglHkBtw

The most powerful frequency of the universe 999 Hz - you will feel God within you healing

https://www.youtube.com/watch?v=-pu93aq9uP4

Emotional And Spiritual Cleansing | Native American Flute Music | Release Melatonin And Toxin

https://www.youtube.com/watch?v=pUCe_F2XUdw

Here is a gentle reminder: Spirituality is a personal journey. It requires time, practice, and patience. The feeling of wholeness will flow down over you and wrap you in a delightful sense of awe.

CHAPTER 10

SPIRITUALITY AND ESSENTIAL OILS

The use of oils for healing and spiritual purposes has a long and rich history dating back thousands of years. The Ancient Egyptians incorporated oils as an integral part of their religious and spiritual practices. Two oils, Frankincense and Myrrh held a special place in temple ceremonies. The Egyptians believed these two oils connected the physical, and spiritual realms.

The importance of oils held sway in the Ancient Chinese belief system as a means of promoting balance within the body and mind. Ayurvedic practices of India made use of sandalwood oil to aid spiritual focus.

Native Americans used oils from sage and cedar in smudging rituals to cleanse spaces and individuals.

Modern practices of meditation, yoga, and holistic healing use a variety of oils in ceremonies and rituals as well as specific health issues. Actually, it's been throughout history that oils, now called essential oils, have been valued for their healing prosperities, but also for their use in spiritual experiences and connecting to higher states of consciousness.

Essential oils are extracted from plants through several methods. Among the popular methods are the following:

- Steam Distillation—The plant material has steam passed through it and then cooled. As the oil separates from the water, it is collected.
- Cold Press Extraction—This is often used on citrus and involves physically pressing the fruit peelings to get the oil.
- Solvent Extraction and just as the name suggests, solvents are used to dissolve the essential oil from the plants.
- CO_2 Extraction involves the use of carbon dioxide under high pressure to extract the oil from the plants

- The maceration procedure involves the soaking of plant material in a carrier oil to extract the essential oils.

When you select an essential oil, the method of its extraction is a personal choice.

One of the beautiful aspects of essential oils is that they can and do enhance spirituality in several ways. Among these are the following:

- ✓ Essential Oils such as Frankincense and Sandalwood burned or placed in a diffuser promote relaxation, calming, and focus during meditation
- ✓ Lavender Essential Oil and or Cedarwood Essential oil transforms an ordinary space into one that feels special—sacred—conducive to spiritual activities. Making prayers to your Spirit Guide might be something you would do.
- ✓ Bergamot Essential Oil is uplifting and raises one's spirits.

- ✓ Chamomile Essential Oil relieves anxiety thus allowing an emotional balance.
- ✓ Jasmine Essential Oil and Myrrh Essential Oil used as 'anointing' oils can enhance your spiritual intentions

Here is a chart showing Essential Oils, what they do in terms of spirituality, and their vibration levels. Each of these oils can be used in various ways: diffusers, topical applications as long as they are mixed with a carrier oil, or place a few drops in a small dish and place it on a nightstand or desk. Ceremonies are a good place to take advantage of Essential Oils' vibrational frequencies and healing powers.

ESSENTIAL OILS FOR SPIRITUALITY AND THEIR VIBRATION LEVEL

BASIL-BALANCES EMOTIONS, *MEDIUM VIBRATION*
BERGAMOT-OPENS PATHWAYS TO SPIRITUAL GROWTH, *MEDIUM VIBRATION*
CARDAMOM-OPENS THE MIND TO NEW PERSPECTIVES. *MEDIUM VIBRATION*
CEDARWOOD-HELPS CONNECT WITH EARTH AND HIGHER SELF. *HIGH VIBRATION*
CLARY SAGE-ENHANCES SPIRITUAL AWARENESS, *HIGH VIBRATION*
CYPRESS-PROMOTES SPIRITUAL TRANSITION, *MEDIUM TO HIGH VIBRATION*
FRANKINCENSE-DEEPENS SPIRITUAL CONNECTION, *VERY HIGH VIBRATION*
GRAPEFRUIT-PROMOTES POSITIVISM, *HIGH VIBRATIONS*
JASMINE-ENHANCES SPIRITUAL INSIGHT, *MEDIUM VIBRATION*
LAVENDER-INNER PEACE, MEDITATION CALMNESS, *HIGH VIBRATION*
LEMON-CLEANSES THE MIND SO IT IS OPEN TO SPIRITUALITY, *HIGH VIBRATION*
MYRRH-SPIRITUAL TRANSFORMATION, *HIGH VIBRATION*
NEROLI-AIDS SPIRITUALITY, OPENS THE HEART, *HIGH VIBRATION*
PATCHOULI- GROUNDING, SELF-ACCEPTANCE, *MEDIUM VIBRATION*
ROSE- OPENS HEART CHAKRA, PROMOTES LOVE, *VERY HGH VIBRATION*
ROSEMARY-ENHANCES SPIRITUAL AWARENESS, *MEDIUM TO HIGH VIBRATION*
SANDALWOOD-HELPS SPIRITUAL AWAKENING, *MEDIUM VIBRATION*
SWEET ORANGE-DISPELS NEGATIVITY, FOSTERS POSITIVITY, *HIGH VIBRATION*
TEA TREE-PROMOTES CLARITY, *MEDIUM VIBRATION*
YLANG-YLANG-AS A SPIRITUAL AID, IT ENHANCES THE CONNECTION WITH THE HEART, *HIGH VIBRATION*

CEREMONY FOR HEALING OF THE SPIRIT

The following ceremony was originally created by ChatGPT.com, an outstanding Internet AI program. I have modified it somewhat based on my years of creating healing sessions, medicine wheels, and transition spirals The ceremony may be used for a group or by one individual.

Purpose: The primary purpose of this ceremony is to promote healing, connect to nature, and spiritual renewal for you and or group.

Needed Materials:

Essential Oils: I suggest Cedarwood, Lavender, and Frankincense. You are free to choose from the Essential Oils for Spirituality and Their Vibrational Levels list or those that have been recommended by your aromatherapist. The oils should be in their original bottles and capped.

Dried Herbs: A bundle of White Sage or Sweetgrass

A small bowl of water

A large turkey feather (non-Native Americans, by law, may not have eagle feathers.) If a feather is not available use a a fan.

A sea shell or a stone (preferably a stone you found)

A hand-held drum or rattle

A prayer cloth (A small clean hand towel will do)

Setting the Stage:

Choose a natural setting, preferably outdoors. Clean the area of any debris. Define a circular space for participants to stand.

Take the Sage or Sweetgrass bundle, light it, and walk around the area, wafting the smoke throughout the circle. Extinguish the bundle. Set it aside for later use.

Create an altar. Place the prayer cloth in the center of the circle. Arrange the bottles of essential oil, dried herbs, sea shells, stones, and a bowl of water on the cloth. Before the ceremony begins open the essential oil(s) and place five drops into the bowl of water. Return the bottle to its original resting place.

Use any natural foliage to continue the natural setting.

Participants:

If you have others participating, call them to the spirit circle you have created.

Have them form a circle, and hold hands.

Briefly explain to them the purpose of the ceremony.

Begin the ceremony with a prayer (If you don't have one, there will be a short prayer in the Resources.)

If you are not comfortable saying or reciting a prayer, consider making a clear and very specific intention.

Smudging:

Smudging is a sacred ceremony within itself. It involves the following four elements: earth (the herbs), water (the bowl with water), fire (match, lighter), and air (the smoke

Blessing: Typically, a blessing is a positive expression. Its significance varies from

culture to culture and often includes the following:
1. Spiritual Connection—Blessings can create a feeling of being connected to the divine or to the spiritual world
2. Guidance and Protection—People seek blessings for safety, health, and guidance in their life's challenges
3. Gratitude and Recognition—Blessings often express gratitude and appreciation
4. Ritual and Tradition—Blessing plays a central role in rituals that mark important life events, and
5. Encouragement and Support—Blessings provide emotional support, a feeling of hope, and comfort.

Two specific blessings will serve as illustrations of what one can do.

Essential Oil Blessing:

> Have each participant choose the essential oil from the altar they would like to experience:

Explain the healing properties of each oil: Cedar, lavender, and Frankincense.

Place three drops of the selected oil on the individual's wrist and have them rub their wrists together for 20 seconds.

Do this for each participant.

A Water Blessing:

Take the bowl of water that has had the essential oils added and walk to each participant. Have each dip the first two fingers of their dominant hand into the bowl. Then have them place those two fingers on their Third Eye. Gently tap the area three times.

Ask each participant to share their feelings if they would like to.

Repeat the short prayer. Close the session.

Please remember this is a suggestion and may modify it to meet your needs and interests.

ALSO, BY NORMAN W. WILSON

Butterflies and All That Jazz with Drs. James G. Massey and James A. Powell

Windows and Images: An Introduction to the Humanities with Drs. James G. Massey and James A. Powell

The Humanities: Contemporary Images

Shamanism: What It's All About

So, You Think You Want To Be A Buddhist?

Promethean Necessity And Its Implications for Humanity

DUH! The American Educational Disaster

The Sayings of Esaugetuh: the Master of Breath

A Shaman's Journey Revealed Through Poetry with Gavriel Navarro

The Shaman's Quest

The Shaman's Transformation

The Shaman's War

The Shaman's Genesis

The Shaman's Revelations

The Making of a Shaman

Activating Your Spirit Guides

Healing-The Shaman's Way

How to Make Moral and Ethical Decisions: A Guide

Teas Soups and Salads

Reiki: The Instructor's Manual

Shamanic Healing

Shamanic Healing Book II Crystals

Healing-The Shaman's Way: Herbs That Help You Heal Book Three

Healing-The Shaman's Way: Using Essential Oils Book Four

Healing-The Shaman's Way: Using Vibrations To Heal Book Five

COURSES AT UDEMY.COM

Healing-The Shaman's Way

Healing- The Shaman's Way Using Crystals

Healing-The Shaman's Way Using Herbs

Healing-The Shaman's Way Using Essential Oils

Healing-The Shaman's Way Using Vibrations to Heal

Healing-The Shaman's Way Religion vs Spirituality

LECTURES ON YOUTUBE

Protecting Yourself

How To Get What You Really Want

The Seven Attributes of Self-hood

Vibration Healing-The Shaman's Way

The Secret to Spirituality One

The Secret to Spirituality Two

The Secret o Spirituality Three

We are Souls with a Human Body

Help The World Meditate

Using Teas To Heal

Sending Heart Energy

Keeping Your Immune System Strong

The Dowsing Rod- The First Line of Defense

How I Became A Shaman

Fixing Your Big Mouth

Detecting Negative Energy

The Shaman and Illness

Eliminating Discrimination, The Shaman's Way

Healing The World

Healing The Shaman's Way

Determining Your Life's Story

A Need For A New Testament

Mirror, Mirror

Healing-The Shaman's Way Using Rose Essential Oil

Five Things to Heal Yourself

Keep Hydrated

WEBSITE

Healingtheshamansway.com

www.ingramcontent.com/pod-product-compliance
Lightning Source LLC
Chambersburg PA
CBHW071720040426
42446CB00011B/2152